FLY HIGH, JOHN GLENN

THE STORY OF AN
★ AMERICAN HERO ★

BY
KATHLEEN KRULL

ILLUSTRATED BY
MAURIZIO A. C. QUARELLO

HARPER
An Imprint of HarperCollinsPublishers

Many people dream of *flying* . . .
soaring above Earth, *floating* without falling.

John Glenn, a small-town Ohio boy, did more than just dream about flying. Airplanes were his obsession. When he was a child, these flying crafts were very new, first flown in 1903 by Orville and Wilbur Wright.

John was only a little boy when he was inspired to play "airplane" with his friends, zooming around the neighborhood with arms stretched out like wings. He built so many model planes, hanging them from his ceiling, that his bedroom looked

John's parents knew all about his passion. Each night the Glenn family went around the dinner table to talk about their day, and John mostly talked about flying. When John was eight, his father took him up in a real plane for a short ride, and that sparked his lifelong goal.

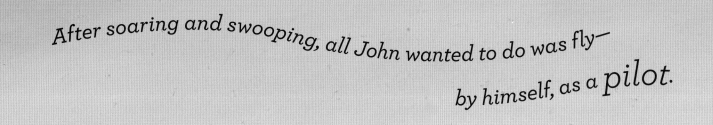

After soaring and swooping, all John wanted to do was fly—

by himself, as a pilot.

John was a boy who lived for adventure, but as he grew older, he became interested in everything—chemistry, music and writing, government and politics. However, his adventurous spirit never went away. All he wanted to do was fly. What he wouldn't give for flying lessons—but they were too expensive for his struggling family.

So he found other ways to "fly." As president of his high school junior class, he made aviation the theme of the junior-senior banquet. He and the other organizers were the "pilots."

His date was his childhood sweetheart, Annie, the daughter of their small-town dentist. Except when she was singing, she had a severe stutter and had trouble speaking. John worked with her, defending her against bullies. Annie supported John's love of flying.

But with no path toward being a pilot, John went off to college to study chemistry.

One night at family dinner, John talked about his day at college—and a brand-new program that was *paying* people to learn how to fly.

His parents, fearing the danger of flying, said absolutely not. John wouldn't give up. He worked hard to change their minds. **And he did!** John earned his flying license at age twenty.

He loved the challenge of sweeping across the sky, the way it absorbed his total attention, all his senses at their peak.

While John mastered the art of flying, Annie was becoming an accomplished musician. In 1941, as he was driving to her senior recital, his car radio erupted with news: the Japanese had attacked America.

Fiercely patriotic, John decided to quit college and enlist in the military. He just wanted to fly, now for his country, and Annie supported him 100 percent.

John served as a distinguished fighter pilot during World War II and afterward. He was awarded multiple medals. A fellow pilot called him "absolutely fearless."

While John was away, he wrote to Annie almost every day. After they married and had children—Dave and Lyn—he named his plane *Lyn Annie Dave*. John hated the thought of worrying Annie. Whenever he left on a scary mission, he would say, "Well, I'm going down to the corner drugstore to buy some gum." It was a silly line stuck in his memory, his way of making light of the danger he faced.

But Annie always played along, replying in the same spirit, "Well, don't take too long."

John never stopped flying. He went from being a war hero to becoming a test pilot for the military, experimenting with exciting new technology. On one mission, he made history. He flew the first supersonic flight across the United States—from California to New York City—in under three and a half hours. The mission brought him his fifth Distinguished Flying Cross. Even better: his family awaited him with cheers and hugs. He had carried his son Dave's Boy Scout knife and his daughter Lyn's jeweled cat pin with him so they could have supersonic souvenirs.

All John had ever wanted to do was fly, and by now he had nearly nine thousand hours of flying time, more than just about any other pilot.

Then came the possibility of space travel, and with it the *Sputnik* crisis. In 1957, the Soviet Union successfully launched a satellite named *Sputnik 1* into outer space.

Americans were shocked! So far, *our* attempts at exploring outer space had failed. Now we were in a space race, and we were losing.

The National Aeronautics and Space Administration (NASA) rushed to start Project Mercury, a bold mission to launch a man into orbit. The first star voyagers—called astronauts—would be chosen from among the nation's 508 test pilots.

John Glenn, test pilot extraordinaire, began reading everything about outer space he could find. It didn't matter that a space mission couldn't have been riskier.

He just wanted to fly, even if it was into the unknown.

Whenever he was home, John and Annie had their own candlelit family dinners, discussing daily events. As always, she supported his new goal—even though "astronaut" was such a new word that she had to look up how to spell it.

Like all the other pilots, John endured test after test to check his readiness for space. Doctors inspected his every nook and cranny, with seventeen tests of his eyes alone. He was heated, frozen, whirled, and stressed.

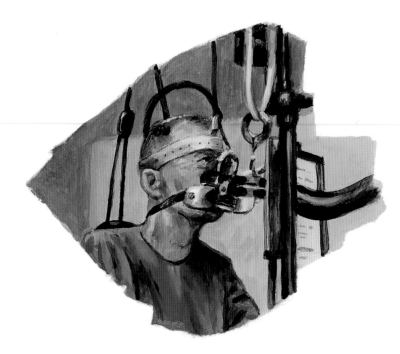

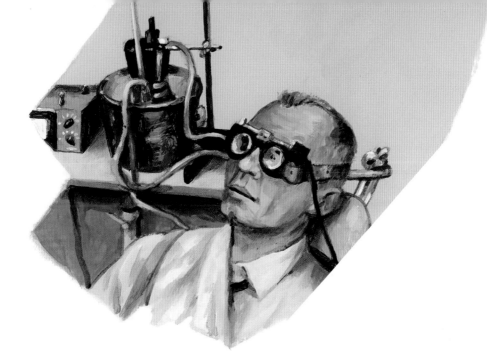

He was also tested mentally, with 566 questions to determine his steadiness. He never showed frustration. Even when isolated for hours in a pitch-black room with a desk and paper, he passed the time writing down eighteen pages of his thoughts, using his finger to keep track of every line.

Over the next months, the number of candidates dropped from 508 test pilots to 110, then to 35. Finally, it was down to 7—the Mercury Seven.

And John was one of them! He was going to get his chance to fly into space.

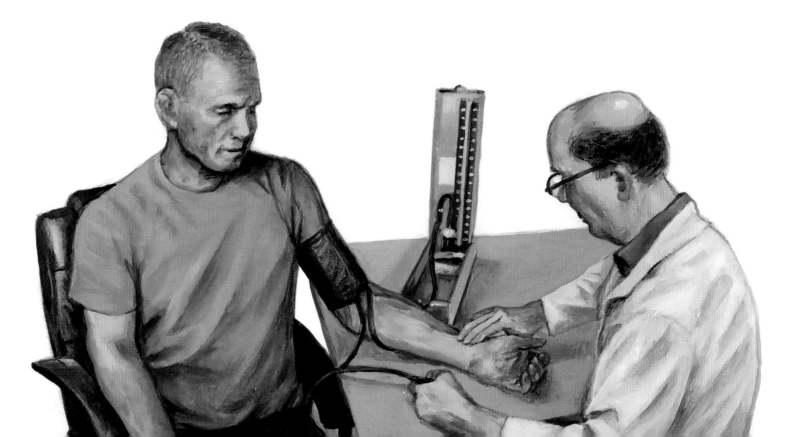

John was elated to plunge into two years of training, pushing his body to its limits. He was becoming more than a pilot—he was now a scientific observer, laying groundwork for future space explorers.

Of great concern was weightlessness, the absence of weight in the vacuum of space. Being weightless could affect a human body in dozens of ways, mostly disagreeable. To prove he wouldn't get spacesick, John spent hours spinning around in a machine that rotated him in three different directions at the same time.

Even as he trained, the Soviet Union kept making successful space launches, and the United States continued to lose the space race.

But John never doubted his mission for a minute.

More than ever, all he wanted to do was fly.

On the ground, the huge NASA team worked to make sure that he would fly safely.

The spacecraft was the most complex machine ever built. To survive extreme vibrations and temperatures as high as 3,000 degrees, it contained seven miles of wire and many thousands of parts—one of the most important being the heat shield to protect the capsule from burning up. Everything—valves, pumps, batteries, timers, sensors—had to be as tiny as possible, not adding any extra weight.

Friendship 7

February 1962 calendar

SUN	MON	TUES	WED	THURS	FRI	SAT
☽	☺	☾	●	1	2	3
4	5	6	7	8	9	10
11	12	13	14	15	16	17
18	19	20	21	22	23	24
25	26	27	28			

Finally, in 1962, John's moment arrived. He called his capsule *Friendship 7*—he named it himself after talking with his kids.

He fiercely wanted to fly—to get a **"Go"** from ground control. But the operation was out of his control. A piece of equipment would break, or bad weather would interfere. So he had to endure one **"No Go"** after another.

But John stayed focused, studying weather maps and star charts, going over all his tasks, avoiding anyone with a sniffle to make sure he didn't get sick. He got his hair trimmed again—space in the capsule was so precious that even his hair had to be minimal.

After eleven delays, he finally heard good news when he woke up at 2:20 a.m. on February 20, 1962. Clouds were thick, but the weather was predicted to clear.

At long last, the mission was a **"Go."**

John needed help putting on his silver space suit, so snug that it required twenty-seven zippers. His boots got laced up, his helmet attached, his gloves tightened. He wiggled his way into the cramped capsule.

He shook the hands of the crew and one last astronaut, and the hatch door closed.

Annie's voice came over his headset. As always, John told her, "Hey, honey, don't be scared. Remember, I'm just going down to the corner drugstore to get a pack of gum."

As always, she replied, "Well, don't take too long."

John heard beeps that meant he was being disconnected from Earth.

"Mercury is go!"

"Engines start!"

"*Ten . . .*

nine . . .

eight . . .

seven . . .

six . . .

five . . .

four . . .

three . . .

two . . .

one . . .

ZERO!"

He heard a thunder-like roar from the bottom of the rocket.

The rocket began its climb and picked up speed, thick smoke mushrooming out from underneath.

"Liftoff!"

Everyone held their breath—at Cape Canaveral and around the world—as the rocket zoomed, launching his two-ton capsule into the sky.

"We're under way!" John said, beginning his conversation with ground control.

"A little bumpy," he said as he felt the capsule vibrate. "Smoothing out real fine . . . flight very smooth now."

Entering Earth's orbit, he called it an "exhilarating surge of up and away."

With each beat of his heart, John soared three miles farther into space.

He felt utterly alone, but he quickly loosened his straps and got busy on his tasks. His flight plan unfurled on a tiny scroll, a bit at a time.

With a jolt, he went weightless. Having no pressure on his body relieved the tightness of his space suit. He found the sensation "extremely pleasant."

But the only time weightlessness foiled him was when he had to change the film on his camera. The roll slipped from his fingers. It went sailing off and he never saw it again.

He cruised over the Atlantic Ocean. Minutes after liftoff, he was marveling at immense dust storms below, swirling through the desert sand of the African continent.

Communication stations all across Earth kept track of his progress. Millions were glued to TVs or listening to radios. From their home, Annie waited with their kids, now ages fourteen and sixteen, and their dog, Chipper.

John had been cleared to orbit Earth three times. So he was set to fly across different time zones on Earth three times. That meant multiple sunsets—and he adored sunsets.

His first one, over the Indian Ocean, came forty minutes into the flight and lasted five precious minutes. Words to describe it seemed weak, but he tried: "A fabulous display," he called it. "I still have a brilliant blue band clear across the horizon. . . . The sky above is absolutely black, completely black."

As the almost-full moon rose behind him, he saw his first stars—fields of them teeming in every direction for hundreds of miles.

He was truly a star voyager, sailing into the night.

He headed toward Australia, where people in one city turned on every light—house, car, and streetlights—welcoming him through the darkness.

He flew over the Pacific Ocean. An hour and fifteen minutes into his journey, he was suddenly surrounded by luminous yellow-green dots. He told ground control, but no one seemed to care. They were more concerned that, over Mexico, the capsule drifted back and forth in a way it wasn't supposed to, wasting fuel. This forced John to take over the controls himself. It wasn't an emergency—yet. Instead, it was proof that having a person on board was crucial to the mission.

He had to cut back on his tasks, but it was a high point of the day: he was flying his own craft, propelling his own body through outer space.

As he passed the two-hour mark, he surged into his second orbit of Earth and his second, rainbow-saturated sunset.

But again, something was worrying those on the ground. A switch showed that the heat shield was loose. If it came off, the spacecraft could explode as it returned to Earth. Ground control decided not to tell John. They didn't want him to panic.

Instead, they instructed him to use other equipment to try to head off the problem. John was confused but followed orders.

All seemed well as he flew over Cape Canaveral and into his third orbit. Clouds broke and he could see the whole state of Florida, bathed in sunshine, then the Mississippi Delta, North Carolina, then islands off Cuba. . . .

With delight he watched the dazzling third sunset, with bands of orange, yellow, blue, and black.

Then, more than four hours since liftoff, he flew over western Australia and headed for Hawaii. It was time to gear up for his return.

Landing safely was one of the most hazardous parts of the mission. His job was to make sure his capsule was coming in at the correct angle as it slowed down.

Then, suddenly, the radio cut out for five long minutes. Everyone feared the worst—that something had happened to John.

Instead of being alarmed, he enjoyed the silence until the radio kicked back in. But as he vibrated violently, he saw burning chunks all around—material breaking off the capsule. It was the only time he was really uncomfortable—the capsule heated up so

To the great relief of all, *Friendship 7* plunged into the Atlantic Ocean safely.

John crawled out of the hatch and made it onto the ship sent to pick him up. A tall glass of ice tea was waiting for him.

It was early afternoon, four hours and fifty-six minutes since he'd taken off.

"I was back with people again," he said.

The next day he was reunited with Annie and their two children. He gave them small American flags he had carried with him so they could have outer space souvenirs. He was engulfed in hugs and afterward was seen wiping his eyes.

He called the mission the **best day of his life.**

It was a good day for the country too,
the most marvelous *of morale boosts.*
John Glenn had become the first American to orbit Earth, majestically circling it three times. He was the epic hero who with his journey had saved the American dream. He had lit up a path toward a sparkling future: "We are now on the verge of a new era."

For the rest of his life, everywhere he went he was greeted with cheers and applause, and when he spoke people cried with emotion.

John never stopped wanting to fly, but he also never stopped serving his country. With strong opinions on science and technology and other issues, he decided to run for a seat in government. He won the election to the United States Senate in 1974.

Always, his special cause was space travel. He strongly opposed any cutbacks to NASA budgets. In 1998, *still* wanting to fly, he campaigned hard to be a crew member aboard the *Discovery* space shuttle. **And he won!** At age seventy-seven he became the oldest person to fly in space.

He didn't stop flying until he was ninety years old.

Today, schools and places all over America are named for John Glenn, the hero who flew into American history.

John Herschel Glenn Jr. was born on July 18, 1921, in the small town of Cambridge, Ohio, with the family moving to New Concord, Ohio, shortly after his birth.

Few Americans have ever experienced as much love. Right after his Mercury mission, he met President John F. Kennedy and was honored with a gigantic ticker-tape parade in New York City.

It had taken a team of eighteen thousand people to make the mission work, including three all-important African American women computing the arc of his descent. Glenn always gave the others credit: "I'm getting the attention for all the thousands of you who worked on it," he told them.

He had lost five pounds during the mission, from dehydration, but he was fine. His only injury was scraped knuckles from accidentally hitting the hatch handle.

After the flight, the heat shield was found to be okay—instead, the switch was faulty. John completely disagreed with ground control's decision not to tell him; he felt pilots had to know all the facts, good or bad.

As for the mysterious dancing lights, they turned out to be floating ice crystals that had been frozen to the capsule.

MORE ABOUT

With all the attention, it was hard to keep his head, but he kept reminding himself he was just a small-town boy from New Concord, Ohio. He always introduced his wife, Annie, as "the real rock in the family."

In 1973, Annie learned about a new approach to help with her stuttering. With hours of hard work every day, she was able to overcome her stutter. (One of her first statements: "John, I've wanted to tell you this for years: Pick up your socks.") Annie went on to give speeches and become a professor of speech pathology.

While serving as a senator from Ohio for over twenty-four years, he cast vote after vote on matters that came before the Senate, almost ten thousand votes in all. After retirement from the Senate, John worked to inspire young people into a life of government service. In 1998, John and Annie helped found what became the John Glenn College of Public Affairs at Ohio State University. He was a professor there, keeping chocolate bars on hand to feed his students.

When he died on December 8, 2016, at age ninety-five, John Glenn had devoted seventy-fours years to serving his country.

JOHN GLENN

★ 1921–2016 ★

★ TIMELINE ★

1921
John Glenn born in Cambridge, Ohio, moving two years later to New Concord.

1954
Becomes test pilot for the navy and the Marines, breaking the transcontinental speed record in 1957.

May 5, 1961
Alan Shepard becomes the first American in space, making a fifteen-minute flight.

1941
Earns pilot's license and drops out of college to enlist in the fight in World War II and later the Korean War.

1959
NASA selects seven candidates for the first U.S. space flights—John Glenn, Scott Carpenter, Gordon Cooper, Gus Grissom, Wally Schirra, Alan Shepard, and Donald Slayton—and they begin training.

1943
Marries Annie Castor and later has two children, David (born 1945) and Lyn (1947).

1957
The Soviet Union's *Sputnik 1* becomes the first satellite in space; *Sputnik 2* successfully orbits the first animal (a dog named Laika) in space; America's first attempt at putting a satellite into orbit fails.

1939
Enters Muskingum College in New Concord, Ohio; after the war receives a bachelor of science degree in engineering as well as an honorary doctor of science degree.

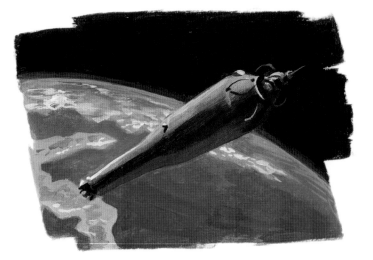

April 12, 1961
The first man in space (Soviet Union's Yuri Gagarin) orbits Earth once.

February 20, 1962
U.S. Marine Lieutenant Colonel astronaut John Glenn becomes the first American to orbit Earth.

2011
America's space shuttle program ends, much to the disapproval of Glenn.

2018
Private companies energize the space race—like Elon Musk's SpaceX, Richard Branson's Virgin Galactic, and Jeff Bezos's Blue Origin (its rocket, scheduled to launch before 2020, is named the *New Glenn*, after John).

1969
Neil Armstrong and Buzz Aldrin become the first men on the moon.

1998
On space shuttle *Discovery*, Glenn becomes the oldest man to be launched into space; over his nine days in orbit he studies the effects of weightlessness on the aging body and does other research.

1965
Begins career as public speaker and executive at Royal Crown Cola, working for political candidates he supports.

1974
Elected to United States Senate.

1999
Retires from Senate and establishes an institute to get young people interested in serving their country.

May 25, 1961
President John F. Kennedy challenges the country to put a man on the moon by the end of the decade.

2016
John Glenn dies at age ninety-five on December 8; American Scott Kelly and Russian Mikhail Kornienko return to Earth after 340 days at the International Space Station, the longest recorded time in space.

BIBLIOGRAPHY

Carpenter, M. Scott, L. Gordon Cooper, Jr.,
John H. Glenn Jr., Virgil I. Grissom,
Walter M. Schirra Jr., Alan B. Shepard Jr.,
and Donald K. Slayton. *We Seven: By the
Astronauts Themselves.* New York: Simon
and Schuster, 1962.

Cole, Michael D. *John Glenn: Astronaut and
Senator*, revised edition. Berkeley Hills, NJ:
Enslow, 2000.

Collard, Sneed B. *John Glenn: Hooked on Flying.*
Tarrytown, NY: Marshall Cavendish, 2009.

Gibbs, Nancy, ed. *John Glenn: A Hero's Life
1921–2016*, Time Commemorative Edition.
New York: Time Inc. Books, 2016.

Glenn, John. *John Glenn: A Memoir.* With Nick
Taylor. New York: Bantam, 1999.

The John Glenn College of Public Affairs.
http://glenn.osu.edu

The John and Annie Glenn Museum.
http://johnglennhome.org

Kennedy Space Center.
https://www.kennedyspacecenter.com

Koppel, Lily. *The Astronaut Wives Club:
A True Story.* New York: Grand Central
Publishing, 2013.

Shetterly, Margot Lee. *Hidden Figures:
The American Dream and the Untold
Story of the Black Women Mathematicians
Who Helped Win the Space Race.*
New York: William Morrow, 2016.

Smithsonian National Air and Space Museum.
https://airandspace.si.edu

Wolfe, Tom. *The Right Stuff.* New York: Farrar,
Straus and Giroux, 1979.

ISBN 978-0-06-274714-3

The artist used oil paints to create the illustrations for this book.
Typography by Erin Fitzsimmons
19 20 21 22 23 SCP 10 9 8 7 6 5 4 3 2 1
❖
First Edition